Morals of the Manichaeans

Morals of the Manichaeans

St. Augustine

Morals of the Manichaeans
© Lighthouse Publishing 2018

Written by: St. Augustine (Nov.13 354 – Aug.28 430)

Translated by: Rev. Richard Stothert, M.A.

Updated into Modern U.S English by A.M. Overett (b. 1960)

All rights reserved. Without limiting the rights under copyright reserved above, no part of this publication may be reproduced, stored in a retrieval system, or transmitted, in any form or by any means (electronic, mechanical, photocopying, recording or otherwise), without the prior written permission of the copyright owner of this book.

Published by
Lighthouse Christian Publishing
SAN 257-4330
5531 Dufferin Drive
Savage, Minnesota, 55378
United States of America

www.lighthousechristianpublishing.com

Introductory Notice. (a.d 388)

Containing a particular refutation of the doctrine of these heretics regarding the origin and nature of evil; an exposure of their pretended symbolical customs of the mouth, of the hands, and of the breast; and a condemnation of their superstitious abstinence and unholy mysteries. Lastly, some crimes brought to light among the Manichæans are mentioned.

Chapter 1. —The Supreme Good is that Which is Possessed of Supreme Existence.

1. Everyone, I suppose, will allow that the question of things good and evil belongs to moral science, in which such terms are in common use. It is therefore to be wished that men would bring to these inquiries such a clear intellectual perfection as might enable them to see the chief good, than which nothing is better or higher, next in order to which comes a rational soul in a state of purity and perfection. If this were clearly understood, it would also become evident that the chief good is that which is properly described as having supreme and original existence. For that exists in the highest sense of the word which continues always the same, which is throughout like itself, which cannot in any part be corrupted or changed, which is not subject to time, which admits of no variation in its present as compared with its former condition. This is existence in its true sense. For in this signification of the word existence there is implied a nature which is self-contained, and which continues immutably. Such things can be said only of God, to whom there is nothing contrary in the strict sense of the word. For the contrary of existence is non-existence. There is therefore no nature contrary to God. But since the minds with which we approach the study of these subjects have their vision damaged and dulled by silly notions, and by perversity of will, let us try as we can to gain some little knowledge of this great matter by degrees and with caution, making our inquiries not like men able to see, but like men groping the dark.

Chapter 2. —What Evil is. That Evil is that Which is Against Nature. In Allowing This, the Manichæans Refute Themselves.

2. You Manichæans often, if not in every case, ask those whom you try to bring over to your heresy, Whence is evil? Suppose I had now met you for the first time, I would ask you, if you please, to follow my example in putting aside for a little the explanation you suppose yourselves to have got of these subjects, and to commence this great inquiry with me as if for the first time. You ask me, Whence is evil? I ask you in return, What is evil? Which is the more reasonable question? Are those right who ask whence a thing is, when they do not know what it is; or he who thinks it necessary to inquire first what it is, in order to avoid the gross absurdity of searching for the origin of a thing unknown? Your answer is quite correct, when you say that evil is that which is contrary to nature; for no one is so mentally blind as not to see that, in every kind, evil is that which is contrary to the nature of the kind. But the establishment of this doctrine is the overthrow of your heresy. For evil is no nature, if it is contrary to nature. Now, according to you, evil is a certain nature and substance. Moreover, whatever is contrary to nature must oppose nature and seek its destruction. For nature means nothing else than that which anything is conceived of as being in its own kind. Hence is the new word which we now use derived from the word for being, —essence namely, or, as we usually say, substance, —while before these words were in use, the word nature was used instead. Here, then, if you will consider the matter without stubbornness, we see that evil is that which falls away from essence and tends

to non-existence.

3. Accordingly, when the Catholic Church declares that God is the author of all natures and substances, those who understand this understand at the same time that God is not the author of evil. For how can He who is the cause of the being of all things be at the same time the cause of their not being, —that is, of their falling off from essence and tending to non-existence? For this is what reason plainly declares to be the definition of evil. Now, how can that race of evil of yours, which you make the supreme evil, be against nature, that is, against substance, when it, according to you, is itself a nature and substance? For if it acts against itself, it destroys its own existence; and when that is completely done, it will come at last to be the supreme evil. But this cannot be done, because you will have it not only to be, but to be everlasting. That cannot then be the chief evil which is spoken of as a substance.

4. But what am I to do? I know that many of you can understand nothing of all this. I know, too, that there are some who have a good understanding and can see these things, and yet are so stubborn in their choice of evil, —a choice that will ruin their understanding as well, —that they try rather to find what reply they can make in order to impose upon inactive and feeble minds, instead of giving their assent to the truth. Still I shall not regret having written either what one of you may come someday to consider impartially, and be led to abandon your error, or what men of understanding and in allegiance to God, and who are still untainted with your errors, may read and so be kept from being led astray by your addresses.

Chapter 3. —If Evil is Defined as that Which is Hurtful, This Implies Another Refutation of the Manichæans.

5. Let us then inquire more carefully, and, if possible, more plainly. I ask you again, What is evil? If you say it is that which is hurtful, here, too, you will not answer amiss. But consider, I pray you; be on your guard, I beg of you; be so good as to lay aside party spirit, and make the inquiry for the sake of finding the truth, not of getting the better of it. Whatever is hurtful takes away some good from that to which it is hurtful; for without the loss of good there can be no hurt. What, I appeal to you, can be plainer than this? what more intelligible? What else is required for complete demonstration to one of average understanding, if he is not perverse? But, if this is granted, the consequence seems plain. In that race which you take for the chief evil, nothing can be liable to be hurt, since there is no good in it. But if, as you assert, there are two natures,—the kingdom of light and the kingdom of darkness; since you make the kingdom of light to be God, attributing to it an uncompounded nature, so that it has no part inferior to another, you must grant, however decidedly in opposition to yourselves, you must grant, nevertheless, that this nature, which you not only do not deny to be the chief good, but spend all your strength in trying to show that it is so, is immutable, incorruptible, impenetrable, inviolable, for otherwise it would not be the chief good; for the chief good is that than which there is nothing better, and for such a nature to be hurt is impossible. Again, if, as has been shown, to hurt is to deprive of good, there can be no hurt to the kingdom of darkness, for there is no good in it. And as

the kingdom of light cannot be hurt, as it is inviolable, what can the evil you speak of be hurtful to?

Chapter 4. —The Difference Between What is Good in Itself and What is Good by Participation.

6. Now, compare with this perplexity, from which you cannot escape, the consistency of the statements in the teaching of the Catholic Church, according to which there is one good which is good supremely and in itself, and not by the participation of any good, but by its own nature and essence; and another good which is good by participation, and by having something bestowed. Thus, it has its being as good from the supreme good, which, however, is still self-contained, and loses nothing. This second kind of good is called a creature, which is liable to hurt through falling away. But of this falling away God is not the author, for He is author of existence and of being. Here we see the proper use of the word evil; for it is correctly applied not to essence, but to negation or loss. We see, too, what nature it is which is liable to hurt. This nature is not the chief evil, for when it is hurt it loses good; nor is it the chief good, for its falling away from good is because it is good not intrinsically, but by possessing the good. And a thing cannot be good by nature when it is spoken of as being made, which shows that the goodness was bestowed. Thus, on the one hand, God is the good, and all things which He has made are good, though not so good as He who made them. For what madman would venture to require that the works should equal the workman, the creatures the Creator? What more do you want? Could you wish for anything plainer than this?

Chapter 5.—If Evil is Defined to Be Corruption, This Completely Refutes the Manichæan Heresy.

7. I ask a third time, What is evil? Perhaps you will reply, Corruption. Undeniably this is a general definition of evil; for corruption implies opposition to nature, and also hurt. But corruption exists not by itself, but in some substance which it corrupts; for corruption itself is not a substance. So the thing which it corrupts is not corruption, is not evil; for what is corrupted suffers the loss of integrity and purity. So that which has no purity to lose cannot be corrupted; and what has, is necessarily good by the participation of purity. Again, what is corrupted is perverted; and what is perverted suffers the loss of order, and order is good. To be corrupted, then, does not imply the absence of good; for in corruption it can be deprived of good, which could not be if there was the absence of good. Therefore that race of darkness, if it was destitute of all good, as you say it was, could not be corrupted, for it had nothing which corruption could take from it; and if corruption takes nothing away, it does not corrupt. Say now, if you dare, that God and the kingdom of God can be corrupted, when you cannot show how the kingdom of the devil, such as you make it, can be corrupted.

Chapter 6. —What Corruption Affects and What It is.

8. What further does the Catholic light say? What do you suppose, but what is the actual truth, that it is the created substance which can be corrupted, for the

uncreated, which is the chief good, is incorruptible; and corruption, which is the chief evil, cannot be corrupted; besides, that it is not a substance? But if you ask what corruption is, consider to what it seeks to bring the things which it corrupts; for it affects those things according to its own nature. Now all things by corruption fall away from what they were, and are brought to non-continuance, to non-existence; for existence implies continuance. Thus the supreme and chief existence is so called because it continues in itself, or is self-contained. In the case of a thing changing for the better, the change is not from continuance, but from perversion to the worse, that is, from falling away from essence; the author of which falling away is not He who is the author of the essence. So in some things there is change for the better, and so a tendency towards existence. And this change is not called a perversion, but reversion or conversion; for perversion is opposed to orderly arrangement. Now things which tend towards existence tend towards order, and, attaining order they attain existence, as far as that is possible to a creature. For order reduces to a certain uniformity that which it arranges; and existence is nothing else than being one. Thus, so far as anything acquires unity, so far it exists. For uniformity and harmony are the effects of unity, and by these compound things exist as far as they have existence. For simple things exist by themselves, for they are one. But things not simple imitate unity by the agreement of their parts; and so far as they attain this, so far they exist. This arrangement is the cause of existence, disorder of non-existence; and perversion or corruption are the other names for disorder. So whatever is corrupted tends to non-existence. You may now be left to reflect upon the effect of corruption, that you may

Morals of the Manichaeans

discover what is the chief evil; for it is that which corruption aims at accomplishing.

Chapter 7. —The Goodness of God Prevents Corruption from Bringing Anything to Non-Existence. The Difference Between Creating and Forming.

9. But the goodness of God does not permit the accomplishment of this end, but so orders all things that fall away that they may exist where their existence is most suitable, till in the order of their movements they return to that from which they fell away. Thus, when rational souls fall away from God, although they possess the greatest amount of freewill, He ranks them in the lower grades of creation, where their proper place is. So they suffer misery by the divine judgment, while they are ranked suitably to their deserts. Hence, we see the excellence of that saying which you are always inveighing against so strongly, "I make good things, and create evil things." To create is to form and arrange. So in some copies it is written, "I make good things and form evil things." To make is used of things previously not in existence; but to form is to arrange what had some kind of existence, so as to improve and enlarge it. Such are the things which God arranges when He says, "I form evil things," meaning things which are falling off, and so tending to non-existence, —not things which have reached that to which they tend. For it has been said, Nothing is allowed in the providence of God to go the length of non-existence.165

10. These things might be discussed more fully and at greater length, but enough has been said for our purpose in dealing with you. We have only to show you the gate which you despair of finding, and make the

uninstructed despair of it too. You can be made to enter only by good-will, on which the divine mercy bestows peace, as the song in the Gospel says, "Glory to God in the highest, and on earth peace to men of good-will." It is enough, I say, to have shown you that there is no way of solving the religious question of good and evil, unless whatever is, as far as it is, is from God; while as far as it falls away from being it is not of God, and yet is always ordered by Divine Providence in agreement with the whole system. If you do not yet see this, I know nothing else that I can do but to discuss the things already said with greater particularity. For nothing save piety and purity can lead the mind to greater things.

Chapter 8. —Evil is Not a Substance, But a Disagreement Hostile to Substance.

11. For what other answer will you give to the question, What is evil? but either that it is against nature, or that it is hurtful, or that it is corruption, or something similar? But I have shown that in these replies you make shipwreck of your cause, unless, indeed, you will answer in the childish way in which you generally speak to children, that evil is fire, poison, a wild beast, and so on. For one of the leaders of this heresy, whose instructions we attended with great familiarity and frequency, used to say with reference to a person who held that evil was not a substance, "I should like to put a scorpion in the man's hand, and see whether he would not withdraw his hand; and in so doing he would get a proof, not in words but in the thing itself, that evil is a substance, for he would not deny that the animal is a substance." He said this not in the presence of the person, but to us, when we repeated to

him the remark which had troubled us, giving, as I said, a childish answer to children. For who with the least tincture of learning or science does not see that these things hurt by disagreement with the bodily temperament, while at other times they agree with it, so as not only not to hurt, but to produce the best effects? For if this poison were evil in itself, the scorpion itself would suffer first and most. In fact, if the poison were quite taken from the animal, it would die. So for its body it is evil to lose what it is evil for our body to receive; and it is good for it to have what it is good for us to want. Is the same thing then both good and evil? By no means; but evil is what is against nature, for this is evil both to the animal and to us. This evil is the disagreement, which certainly is not a substance, but hostile to substance. Whence then is it? See what it leads to, and you will learn, if any inner light lives in you. It leads all that it destroys to non-existence. Now God is the author of existence; and there is no existence which, as far as it is existing, leads to non-existence: Thus we learn whence disagreement is not; as to whence it is, nothing can be said.

12. We read in history of a female criminal in Athens, who succeeded in drinking the quantity of poison allotted as a fatal draught for the condemned with little or no injury to her health, by taking it at intervals. So being condemned, she took the poison in the prescribed quantity like the rest, but rendered it powerless by accustoming herself to it, and did not die like the rest. And as this excited great wonder, she was banished. If poison is an evil, are we to think that she made it to be no evil to her? What could be more absurd than this? But because disagreement is an evil, what she did was to make the poisonous matter agree with her own body by a process of

habituation. For how could she by any amount of cunning have brought it about that disagreement should not hurt her? Why so? Because what is truly and properly an evil is hurtful both always and to all. Oil is beneficial to our bodies, but very much the opposite to many six-footed animals. And is not hellebore sometimes food, sometimes medicine, and sometimes poison. Does not everyone maintain that salt taken in excess is poisonous? And yet the benefits to the body from salt are innumerable and most important. Sea-water is injurious when drunk by land animals, but it is most suitable and useful to many who bathe their bodies in it and to fish it is useful and wholesome in both ways. Bread nourishes man, but kills hawks. And does not mud itself, which is offensive and noxious when swallowed or smelt, serve as cooling to the touch in hot weather, and as a cure for wounds from fire? What can be nastier than dung, or more worthless than ashes? And yet they are of such use to the fields, that the Romans thought divine honors due to the discoverer, Stercutio, from whose name the word for dung [stercus] is derived.

13. But why enumerate details which are countless? We need not go farther than the four elements themselves, which, as everyone knows, are beneficial when there is agreement, and bitterly opposed to nature when there is disagreement in the objects acted upon. We who live in air die under earth or under water, while innumerable animals creep alive in sand or loose earth, and fish die in our air. Fire consumes our bodies, but, when suitably applied, it both restores from cold, and expels diseases without number. The sun to which you bow the knee, and than which, indeed, there is no fairer object among visible things, strengthens the eyes of

eagles, but hurts and dims our eyes when we gaze on it; and yet we too can accustom ourselves to look upon it without injury. Will you, then, allow the sun to be compared to the poison which the Athenian woman made harmless by habituating herself to it? Reflect for once, and consider that if a substance is an evil because it hurts someone, the light which you worship cannot be acquitted of this charge. See the preferableness of making evil in general to consist in this disagreement, from which the sun's ray produces dimness in the eyes, though nothing is pleasanter to the eyes than light.

Chapter 9. —The Manichæan Fictions About Things Good and Evil are Not Consistent with Themselves.

14. I have said these things to make you cease, if that is possible, giving the name of evil to a region boundless in depth and length; to a mind wandering through the region; to the five caverns of the elements,— one full of darkness, another of waters, another of winds, another of fire, another of smoke; to the animals born in each of these elements,—serpents in the darkness, swimming creatures in the waters, flying creatures in the winds, quadrupeds in the fire, bipeds in the smoke. For these things, as you describe them, cannot be called evil; for all such things, as far as they exist, must have their existence from the most high God, for as far as they exist they are good. If pain and weakness is an evil, the animals you speak of were of such physical strength that their abortive offspring, after, as your sect believes, the world was formed of them, fell from heaven to earth, according to you, and could not die. If blindness is an

evil, they could see; if deafness, they could hear. If to be nearly or altogether dumb is an evil, their speech was so clear and intelligible, that, as you assert, they decided to make war against God in compliance with an address delivered in their assembly. If sterility is an evil, they were prolific in children. If exile is an evil, they were in their own country, and occupied their own territories. If servitude is an evil, some of them were rulers. If death is an evil, they were alive, and the life was such that, by your statement, even after God was victorious, it was impossible for the mind ever to die.

15. Can you tell me how it is that in the chief evil so many good things are to be found, the opposites of the evils above mentioned? and if these are not evils, can any substance be an evil, as far as it is a substance? If weakness is not an evil, can a weak body be an evil? If blindness is not an evil, can darkness be an evil? If deafness is not an evil, can a deaf man be an evil? If dumbness is not an evil, can a fish be an evil? If sterility is not an evil, how can we call a barren animal an evil? If exile is not an evil, how can we give that name to an animal in exile, or to an animal sending someone into exile? If servitude is not an evil, in what sense is a subject animal an evil, or one enforcing subjection? If death is not an evil, in what sense is a mortal animal an evil, or one causing death? Or if these are evils, must we not give the name of good things to bodily strength, sight, hearing, persuasive speech, fertility, native land, liberty, life, all which you hold to exist in that kingdom of evil, and yet venture to call it the perfection of evil?

16. Once more, if, as has never been denied, unsuitableness is an evil, what can be more suitable than those elements to their respective animals, —the darkness

to serpents, the waters to swimming creatures, the winds to flying creatures, the fire to voracious animals, the smoke to soaring animals? Such is the harmony which you describe as existing in the race of strife; such the order in the seat of confusion. If what is hurtful is an evil, I do not repeat the strong objection already stated, that no hurt can be suffered where no good exists; but if that is not so clear, one thing at least is easily seen and understood as following from the acknowledged truth, that what is hurtful is an evil. The smoke in that region did not hurt bipeds: it produced them, and nourished and sustained them without injury in their birth, their growth, and their rule. But now, when the evil has some good mixed with it, the smoke has become more hurtful, so that we, who certainly are bipeds, instead of being sustained by it, are blinded, and suffocated, and killed by it. Could the mixture of good have given such destructiveness to evil elements? Could there be such confusion in the divine government?

17. In the other cases, at least, how is it that we find that congruity which misled your author and induced him to fabricate falsehoods? Why does darkness agree with serpents, and waters with swimming creatures, and winds with flying creatures, though the fire burns up quadrupeds, and smoke chokes us? Then, again, have not serpents very sharp sight, and do they not love the sunshine, and abound most where the calmness of the air prevents the clouds from gathering much or often? How very absurd that the natives and lovers of darkness should live most comfortably and agreeably where the clearest light is enjoyed! Or if you say that it is the heat rather than the light that they enjoy, it would be more reasonable to assign to fire serpents, which are naturally of rapid

motion, than the slow-going asp. Besides, all must admit that light is agreeable to the eyes of the asp, for they are compared to an eagle's eyes. But enough of the lower animals. Let us, I pray, attend to what is true of ourselves without persisting in error, and so our minds shall be disentangled from silly and mischievous falsehoods. For is it not intolerable perversity to say that in the race of darkness, where there was no mixture of light, the biped animals had so sound and strong, so incredible force of eyesight, that even in their darkness they could see the perfectly pure light (as you represent it) of the kingdom of God? for, according to you, even these beings could see this light, and could gaze at it, and study it, and delight in it, and desire it; whereas our eyes, after mixture with light, with the chief good, yea, with God, have become so tender and weak, that we can neither see anything in the dark, nor bear to look at the sun, but, after looking, lose sight of what we could see before.

18. The same remarks are applicable if we take corruption to be an evil, which no one doubts. The smoke did not corrupt that race of animals, though it corrupts animals now. Not to go over all the particulars, which would be tedious, and is not necessary, the living creatures of your imaginary description were so much less liable to corruption than animals are now, that their abortive and premature offspring, cast headlong from heaven to earth, both lived and were productive, and could band together again, having, forsooth, their original vigor, because they were conceived before good was mixed with the evil; for, after this mixture, the animals born are, according to you, those which we now see to be very feeble and easily giving way to corruption. Can anyone persist in the belief of error like this, unless he

fails to see these things, or is affected by your habit and association in such an amazing way as to be proof against all the force of reasoning?

Chapter 10. —Three Moral Symbols Devised by the Manichæans for No Good.

19. Now that I have shown, as I think, how much darkness and error is in your opinions about good and evil things in general, let us examine now those three symbols which you extol so highly, and boast of as excellent observances. What then are those three symbols? That of the mouth, that of the hands, and that of the breast. What does this mean? That man, we are told, should be pure and innocent in mouth, in hands, and in breast. But what if he sins with eyes, ears, or nose? What if he hurts someone with his heels, or perhaps kills him? How can he be reckoned criminal when he has not sinned with mouth, hands, or breast? But, it is replied, by the mouth we are to understand all the organs of sense in the head; by the hands, all bodily actions; by the breast, all lustful tendencies. To what, then, do you assign blasphemies? To the mouth or to the hand? For blasphemy is an action of the tongue. And if all actions are to be classed under one head, why should you join together the actions of the hands and the feet, and not those of the tongue. Do you wish to separate the action of the tongue, as being for the purpose of expressing something, from actions which are not for this purpose, so that the symbol of the hands should mean abstinence from all evil actions which are not for the purpose of expressing something? But then, what if someone sins by expressing something with his hands, as is done in writing or in some significant

gesture? This cannot be assigned to the tongue and the mouth, for it is done by the hands. When you have three symbols of the mouth, the hands, and the breast, it is quite inadmissible to charge against the mouth sins found in the hands. And if you assign action in general to the hands, there is no reason for including under this the action of the feet and not that of the tongue. Do you see how the desire of novelty, with its attendant error, lands you in great difficulties? For you find it impossible to include purification of all sins in these three symbols, which you set forth as a kind of new classification.

Chapter 11. —The Value of the Symbol of the Mouth Among the Manichæans, Who are Found Guilty of Blaspheming God.

20. Classify as you please, omit what you please, we must discuss the doctrines you insist upon most. You say that the symbol of the mouth implies refraining from all blasphemy. But blasphemy is speaking evil of good things. So usually the word blasphemy is applied only to speaking evil of God; for about man there is uncertainty, but God is without controversy good. If, then, you are proved guilty of saying worse things of God than anyone else says, what becomes of your famous symbol of the mouth? The evidence is not obscure, but clear and obvious to every understanding, and irresistible, the more so that no one can remain in ignorance of it, that God is incorruptible, immutable, liable to no injury, to no want, to no weakness, to no misery. All this the common sense of rational beings perceives, and even you assent when you hear it.

21. But when you begin to relate your fables, that

God is corruptible, and mutable, and subject to injury, and exposed to want and weakness, and not secure from misery, this is what you are blind enough to teach, and what some are blind enough to believe. And this is not all; for, according to you, God is not only corruptible, but corrupted; not only changeable, but changed; not only subject to injury, but injured; not only liable to want, but in want; not only possibly, but actually weak; not only exposed to misery, but miserable. You say that the soul is God, or a part of God. I do not see how it can be part of God without being God. A part of gold is gold; of silver silver; of stone stone; and, to come to greater things, part of earth is earth, part of water is water, and of air air; and if you take part from fire, you will not deny it to be fire; and part of light can be nothing but light. Why then should part of God not be God? Has God a jointed body, like man and the lower animals? For part of man is not man.

22. I will deal with each of these opinions separately. If you view God as resembling light, you must admit that part of God is God. Hence, when you make the soul part of God, though you allow it to be corrupted as being foolish, and changed as having once been wise, and in want as needing health, and feeble as needing medicine, and miserable as desiring happiness, all these things you profanely attribute to God. Or if you deny these things of the mind, it follows that the Spirit is not required to lead the soul into truth, since it is not in folly; nor is the soul renewed by true religion, since it does not need renewal; nor is it perfected by your symbols, since it is already perfect; nor does God give it assistance, since it does not need it; nor is Christ its physician, since it is in health; nor does it require the

promise of happiness in another life. Why then is Jesus called the deliverer, according to His own words in the Gospel, "If the Son shall make you free, ye shall be free indeed?" And the Apostle Paul says, "Ye have been called to liberty." The soul, then, which has not attained this liberty is in bondage. Therefore, according to you, God, since part of God is God, is both corrupted by folly, and is changed by falling, and is injured by the loss of perfection, and needs help, and is weakened by disease, and bowed down with misery, and subject to disgraceful bondage.

23. Again, if part of God is not God, still He is not incorrupt when His part is corrupted, nor unchanged when there is change in any part, nor uninjured when He is not perfect in every part, nor free from want when He is busily endeavoring to recover part of Himself, nor quite whole when He has a weak part, nor perfectly happy when any part is suffering misery, nor entirely free when any part is under bondage. These are conclusions to which you are driven, because you say that the soul, which you see to be in such a calamitous condition, is part of God. If you can succeed in making your sect abandon these and many similar opinions, then you may speak of your mouth being free from blasphemies. Better still, leave the sect; for if you cease to believe and to repeat what Manichæus has written, you will be no longer Manichæans.

24. That God is the supreme good, and that than which nothing can be or can be conceived better, we must either understand or believe, if we wish to keep clear of blasphemy. There is a relation of numbers which cannot possibly be impaired or altered, nor can any nature by any amount of violence prevent the number which comes after

one from being the double of one. This can in no way be changed; and yet you represent God as changeable! This relation preserves its integrity inviolable; and you will not allow God an equality even in this! Let some race of darkness take in the abstract the number three, consisting of indivisible units, and divide it into two equal parts. Your mind perceives that no hostility could effect this. And can that which is unable to injure a numerical relation injure God? If it could not, what possible necessity could there be for a part of him to be mixed with evil, and driven into such miseries?

Chapter 12. —Manichæan Subterfuge.

25. For this gives rise to the question, which used to throw us into great perplexity even when we were your zealous disciples, nor could we find any answer, —what the race of darkness would have done to God, supposing He had refused to fight with it at the cost of such calamity to part of Himself. For if God would not have suffered any loss by remaining quiet, we thought it hard that we had been sent to endure so much. Again, if He would have suffered, His nature cannot have been incorruptible, as it behooves the nature of God to be. Sometimes the answer was, that it was not for the sake of escaping evil or avoiding injury, but that God in His natural goodness wished to bestow the blessing of order on a disturbed and disordered nature. This is not what we find in the Manichæan books: there it is constantly implied and constantly asserted that God guarded against an invasion of His enemies. But supposing this answer, which was given from want of a better, to represent the opinion of the Manichæans, is God, in their view, vindicated from

the charge of cruelty or weakness? For this goodness of His to the hostile race proved most pernicious to His own subjects. Besides, if God's nature could not be corrupted nor changed, neither could any destructive influence corrupt or change us; and the order to be bestowed on the race of strangers might have been bestowed without robbing us of it.

26. Since those times, however, another answer has appeared which I heard recently at Carthage. For one, whom I wish much to see brought out of this error, when reduced to this same dilemma, ventured to say that the kingdom had its own limits, which might be invaded by a hostile race, though God Himself could not be injured. But this is a reply which your founder would never consent to give; for he would be likely to see that such an opinion would lead to a still speedier demolition of his heresy. And in fact any one of average intellect, who hears that in this nature part is subject to injury and part not, will at once perceive that this makes not two but three natures, —one violable, a second inviolable, and a third violating.

Chapter 13. —Actions to Be Judged of from Their Motive, Not from Externals. Manichæan Abstinence to Be Tried by This Principle.

27. Having every day in your mouth these blasphemies which come from your heart, you ought not to continue holding up the symbol of the mouth as something wonderful, to ensnare the ignorant. But perhaps you think the symbol of the mouth excellent and admirable because you do not eat flesh or drink wine. But what is your end in this? For according as the end we

have in view in our actions, because which we do whatever we do, is not only not culpable but also praiseworthy, so only can our actions merit any praise. If the end we have regard to in any performance is unlawful and blameworthy, the performance itself will be unhesitatingly condemned as improper.

28. We are told of Catiline that he could bear cold, thirst, and hunger. This the vile miscreant had in common with our apostles. What then distinguishes the parricide from our apostles but the precisely opposite end which he followed? He bore these things in order to gratify his fierce and ungoverned passions; they, on the other hand, in order to restrain these passions and subdue them to reason. You often say, when you are told of the great number of Catholic virgins, a she-mule is a virgin. This, indeed, is said in ignorance of the Catholic system, and is not applicable. Still, what you mean is that this continence is worthless unless it leads, on right principles, to an end of high excellence. Catholic Christians might also compare your abstinence from wine and flesh to that of cattle and many small birds, as likewise of countless sorts of worms. But, not to be impertinent like you, I will not make this comparison prematurely, but will first examine your end in what you do. For I suppose I may safely take it as agreed on, that in such customs the end is the thing to look to. Therefore, if your end is to be frugal and to restrain the appetite which finds gratification in eating and drinking, I assent and approve. But this is not the case.

29. Suppose, what is quite possible, that there is one so frugal and sparing in his diet, that, instead of gratifying his appetite or his palate, he refrains from eating twice in one day, and at supper takes a little

cabbage moistened and seasoned with lard, just enough to keep down hunger; and quenches his thirst, from regard to his health, with two or three draughts of pure wine; and this is his regular diet: whereas another of different habits never takes flesh or wine, but makes an agreeable repast at two o'clock on rare and foreign vegetables, varied with a number of courses, and well sprinkled with pepper, and sups in the same style towards night; and drinks honey-vinegar, mead, raisin-wine, and the juices of various fruits, no bad imitation of wine, and even surpassing it in sweetness; and drinks not for thirst but for pleasure; and makes this provision for himself daily, and feasts in this sumptuous style, not because he requires it, but only gratifying his taste;—which of these two do you regard as living most abstemiously in food and drink? You cannot surely be so blind as not to put the man of the little lard and wine above this glutton!

30. This is the true view; but your doctrine sounds very differently. For one of your elect distinguished by the three symbols may live like the second person in this description, and though he may be reproved by one or two of the more sedate, he cannot be condemned as abusing the symbols. But should he sup with the other person, and moisten his lips with a morsel of rancid bacon, or refresh them with a drink of spoilt wine, he is pronounced a transgressor of the symbol, and by the judgment of your founder is consigned to hell, while you, though wondering, must assent. Will you not discard these errors? Will you not listen to reason? Will you not offer some little resistance to the force of habit? Is not such doctrine most unreasonable? Is it not insanity? Is it not the greatest absurdity that one, who stuffs and loads his stomach every day to gratify his appetite with

mushrooms, rice, truffles, cake, mead, pepper, and assafœtida, and who fares thus every day, cannot be convicted of transgressing the three symbols, that is, the rule of sanctity; whereas another, who seasons his dish of the commonest herbs with some smoky morsel of meat, and takes only so much of this as is needed for the refreshment of his body, and drinks three cups of wine for the sake of keeping in health, should, for exchanging the former diet for this, be doomed to certain punishment?

Chapter 14.—Three Good Reasons for Abstaining from Certain Kinds of Food.

31. But, you reply, the apostle says, "It is good, brethren, neither to eat flesh, nor to drink wine." No one denies that this is good, provided that it is for the end already mentioned, of which it is said, "Make not provision for the flesh to fulfill the lusts thereof;" or for the ends pointed out by the apostle, namely, either to check the appetite, which is apt to go to a more wild and uncontrollable excess in these things than in others, or lest a brother should be offended, or lest the weak should hold fellowship with an idol. For at the time when the apostle wrote, the flesh of sacrifices was often sold in the market. And because wine, too, was used in libations to the gods of the Gentiles, many weaker brethren, accustomed to purchase such things, preferred to abstain entirely from flesh and wine rather than run the risk of having fellowship, as they considered it, with idols, even ignorantly. And, for their sakes, even those who were stronger, and had faith enough to see the insignificance of these things, knowing that nothing is unclean except from an evil conscience, and holding by the saying of the Lord,

"Not that which entered into your mouth defiled you, but that which cometh out of it," still, lest these weaker brethren should stumble, were bound to abstain from these things. And this is not a mere theory, but is clearly taught in the epistles of the apostle himself. For you are in the habit of quoting only the words, "It is good, brethren, neither to eat flesh, nor to drink wine," without adding what follows, "nor anything whereby thy brother stumbles, or is offended or is made weak." These words show the intention of the apostle in giving the admonition.

32. This is evident from the preceding and succeeding context. The passage is a long one to quote, but, for the sake of those who are indolent in reading and searching the sacred Scriptures, we must give the whole of it. "Him that is weak in the faith," says the apostle, "receive ye, but not to doubtful disputations. For one believeth that he may eat all things: another, who is weak, eats herbs. Let not him that eat despise him that eats not; and let not him that eats not judge him that eats, for God hath received him. Who art thou that judges another man's servant? to his own master he stands or falls; yea, he shall be holded up: for God is able to make him stand. One man esteemed one day above another; another esteemed every day alike. Let every man be fully persuaded in his own mind. He that regarded the day, regarded it to the Lord. He that eats, eats to the Lord, for he giveth God thanks; and he that eats not, to the Lord he eats not, and giveth God thanks. For none of us lives to himself, and no man dies to himself. For whether we live, we live unto the Lord; and whether we die, we die unto the Lord: whether we live, therefore, or die, we are the Lord's. For to this end Christ both lived, and died and rose again, that He might be Lord both of the dead and

living. But why dost thou judge thy brother? or why dost thou set at naught thy brother? for we shall all stand before the judgment-seat of God. For it is written, As I live, saith the Lord, every knee shall bow to me, and every tongue shall confess to God. So, then every one of us shall give account of himself to God. Let us not, therefore, judge one another anymore: but judge this rather, that no man put a stumbling block, or occasion to fall, in his brother's way. I know, and am persuaded in the Lord Jesus, that there is nothing common of itself: but to him that esteemed anything to be common, to him it is common. But if thy brother be grieved with thy meat, now walk thou not charitably. Destroy not him with thy meat, for whom Christ died. Let not then our good be evil spoken of. For the kingdom of God is not meat and drink; but righteousness, and peace, and joy in the Holy Ghost. For he who in this serves Christ is acceptable to God, and approved of men. Let us therefore follow after the things which make for peace, and things whereby one may edify another. For meat destroys not the work of God. All things indeed are pure; but it is evil for that man who eats with offense. It is good neither to eat flesh, nor to drink wine, nor anything whereby thy brother stumbles, or is offended, or is made weak. Hast thou faith? have it to thyself before God. Happy is he who condemns not himself in that thing which he allowed. And he that distinguishes is damned if he eats, because he eats not of faith: for whatsoever is not of faith is sin. We then that are strong ought to bear the infirmities of the weak, and not to please ourselves. Let every one of us please his neighbor for his good to edification. For even Christ pleased not Himself."

33. Is it not clear that what the apostle required

was, that the stronger should not eat flesh nor drink wine, because they gave offense to the weak by not going along with them, and made them think that those who in faith judged all things to be pure, did homage to idols in not abstaining from that kind of food and drink? This is also set forth in the following passage of the Epistle to the Corinthians: "As concerning, therefore, the eating of those things that are offered in sacrifice unto idols, we know that an idol is nothing in the world, and that there is none other God but one. For though there be that are called gods, whether in heaven or in earth, but to us there is but one God, the Father, of whom are all things, and we in Him; and one Lord Jesus Christ, by whom are all things, and we by Him. Howbeit there is not in every man that knowledge: for some, with conscience of the idol unto this hour, eat it as a thing offered to an idol; and their conscience being weak is defiled. But meat commended us not to God: for neither, if we eat, shall we abound; neither, if we eat not, shall we suffer want. But take heed, lest by any means this liberty of yours become a stumbling-block to them that are weak. For if any man sees one who has knowledge sit at meat in the idol's temple, shall not his conscience being weak be emboldened to eat those things which are offered to idols; and through thy knowledge shall the weak brother perish, for whom Christ died? But when ye sin so against the brethren, and wound their weak conscience, ye sin against Christ. Wherefore, if meat make my brother to offend, I will eat no flesh forever, lest I make my brother to offend."

34. Again, in another place: "What say I then? that the idol is anything? or that which is offered in sacrifice to idols is anything? But the things which the

Gentiles sacrifice they sacrifice to devils, and not to God: and I would not that ye should have fellowship with devils. Ye cannot drink the cup of the Lord, and the cup of devils: ye cannot be partakers of the Lord's table and of the table of devils. Do we provoke the Lord to jealousy? are we stronger than He? All things are lawful for me, but all things are not expedient: all things are lawful for me, but all things edify not. Let no man seek his own, but every man what is another's. Whatsoever is sold in the shambles, that eat, asking no question for conscience sake. But if any man says unto you, This is offered in sacrifice unto idols, eat not for his sake that shows it, and for conscience sake: conscience, I say, not thine own, but another's: for why is my liberty judged of another man's conscience? For if I be a partaker with thanksgiving, why am I evil spoken of for that for which I give thanks? Whether, therefore, ye eat or drink, or whatsoever ye do, do all to the glory of God. Give none offence, neither to the Jews, nor to the Greeks, nor to the Church of God: even as I please all men in all things not seeking mine own profit, but the profit of many that they may be saved. Be ye followers of me, even as I also am of Christ."

35. It is clear, then, I think, for what end we should abstain from flesh and wine. The end is threefold: to check indulgence, which is mostly practiced in this sort of food, and in this kind of drink goes the length of intoxication; to protect weakness, because the things which are sacrificed and offered in libation; and, what is most praiseworthy of all, from love, not to offend the weakness of those feebler than ourselves, who abstain from these things. You, again, consider a morsel of meat unclean; whereas the apostle says that all things are clean,

but that it is evil to him that eats with offence. And no doubt you are defiled by such food, simply because you think it unclean. For the apostle says, "I know, and am persuaded by the Lord Jesus, that there is nothing common of itself: but to him that esteemed anything common, to him it is common." And everyone can see that by common he means unclean and defiled. But it is folly to discuss passages of Scripture with you; for you both mislead people by promising to prove your doctrines, and those books which possess authority to demand our homage you affirm to be corrupted by spurious interpolations. Prove then to me your doctrine that flesh defiles the eater, when it is taken without offending any one, without any weak notions, and without any excess.

Chapter 15. —Why the Manichæans Prohibit the Use of Flesh.

36. It is worthwhile to take note of the whole reason for their superstitious abstinence, which is given as follows: —Since, we are told, the member of God has been mixed with the substance of evil, to repress it and to keep it from excessive ferocity, —for that is what you say, —the world is made up of both natures, of good and evil, mixed together. But this part of God is daily being set free in all parts of the world, and restored to its own domain. But in its passage upwards as vapor from earth to heaven, it enters plants, because their roots are fixed in the earth, and so gives fertility and strength to all herbs and shrubs. From these animals get their food, and, where there is sexual intercourse, fetter in the flesh the member of God, and, turning it from its proper course,

they come in the way and entangle it in errors and troubles. So then, if food consisting of vegetables and fruits comes to the saints, that is, to the Manichæans by means of their chastity, and prayers, and psalms, whatever in it is excellent and divine is purified, and so is entirely perfected, in order to restoration, free from all hindrance, to its own domain. Hence you forbid people to give bread or vegetables, or even water, which would cost nobody anything, to a beggar, if he is not a Manichæan, lest he should defile the member of God by his sins, and obstruct its return.

37. Flesh, you say, is made up of pollution itself. For, according to you, some portion of that divine part escapes in the eating of vegetables and fruits: it escapes while they undergo the infliction of rubbing, grinding, or cooking, as also of biting or chewing. It escapes, too, in all motions of animals, in the carriage of burdens, in exercise, in toil, or in any sort of action. It escapes, too, in our rest, when digestion is going on in the body by means of internal heat. And as the divine nature escapes in all these ways, some very unclean dregs remain, from which, in sexual intercourse, flesh is formed. These dregs, however, fly off, in the motions above mentioned, along with what is good in the soul; for though it is mostly, it is not entirely good. So, when the soul has left the flesh, the dregs are utterly filthy, and the soul of those who eat flesh is defiled.

Chapter 16. —Disclosure of the Monstrous Tenets of the Manichæans.

38. O the obscurity of the nature of things! How hard to expose falsehood! Who that hears these things, if

he is one who has not learned the causes of things, and who, not yet illuminated by any ray of truth, is deceived by material images, would not think them true, precisely because the things spoken of are invisible, and are presented to the mind under the form of visible things, and can be eloquently expressed? Men of this description exist in numbers and in droves, who are kept from being led away into these errors more by a fear grounded on religious feeling than by reason. I will therefore endeavor, as God may please to enable me, so to refute these errors, as that their falsehood and absurdity will be manifest not only in the judgment of the wise, who reject them on hearing them, but also to the intelligence of the multitude.

39. Tell me then, first, where you get the doctrine that part of God, as you call it, exists in corn, beans, cabbage, and flowers and fruits. From the beauty of the color, say they, and the sweetness of the taste; this is evident; and as these are not found in rotten substances, we learn that their good has been taken from them. Are they not ashamed to attribute the finding of God to the nose and the palate? But I pass from this. For I will speak, using words in their proper sense; and, as the saying is, this is not so easy in speaking to you. Let us see rather what sort of mind is required to understand this; how, if the presence of good in bodies is shown by their color, the dung of animals, the refuse of flesh itself, has all kinds of bright colors, sometimes white, often golden; and so on, though these are what you take in fruits and flowers as proofs of the presence and indwelling of God. Why is it that in a rose you hold the red color to be an indication of an abundance of good, while the same color in blood you condemn? Why do you regard with pleasure

in a violet the same color which you turn away from in cases of cholera, or of people with jaundice, or in the excrement of infants? Why do you believe the light, shining appearance of oil to be a sign of a plentiful admixture of good, which you readily set about purifying by taking the oil into your throats and stomachs, while you are afraid to touch your lips with a drop of fat, though it has the same shining appearance as oil? Why do you look upon a yellow melon as part of the treasures of God, and not rancid bacon fat or the yolk of an egg? Why do you think that whiteness in a lettuce proclaims God, and not in milk? So much for colors, about which (to mention nothing else) you cannot compare any flower-clad meadow with the wings and feathers of a single peacock, though these are of flesh and of fleshly origin.

40. Again, if this good is discovered also by smell, perfumes of excellent smell are made from the flesh of some animals. And the smell of food, when cooked along with flesh of delicate flavor, is better than if cooked without it. Once more, if you think that the things that have a better smell than others are therefore cleaner, there is a kind of mud which you ought to take to your meals instead of water from the cistern; for dry earth moistened with rain has an odor most agreeable to the sense, and this sort of mud has a better smell than rain-water taken by itself. But if we must have the authority of taste to prove the presence in any object of part of God, he must dwell in dates and honey more than in pork, but more in pork than in beans. I grant that He dwells more in a fig than in a liver; but then you must allow that He is more in liver than in beet. And, on this principle, must you not confess that some plants, which none of you can doubt to be cleaner than flesh, receive God from this very

flesh, if we are to think of God as mixed with the flavor? For both cabbages taste better when cooked along with flesh; and, while we cannot relish the plants on which cattle feed, when these are turned into milk we think them improved in color, and find them very agreeable to the taste.

41. Or must we think that good is to be found in greater quantity where the three good qualities—a good color, and smell, and taste—are found together? Then you must not admire and praise flowers so much, as you cannot admit them to be tried at the tribunal of the palate. At least you must not prefer purslain to flesh, since flesh when cooked is superior in color, smell, and taste. A young pig roasted (for your ideas on this subject force us to discuss good and evil with you as if you were cooks and confectioners, instead of men of reading or literary taste) is bright in color, and agreeable in smell, and pleasant in taste. Here is a perfect evidence of the presence of the divine substance. You are invited by this threefold testimony, and called on to purify this substance by your sanctity. Make the attack. Why do you hold back? What objection have you to make. In color alone the excrement of an infant surpasses lentils; in smell alone a roast morsel surpasses a soft green fig; in taste alone a kid when slaughtered surpasses the plant which it fed on when alive: and we have found a kind of flesh in flavor of which all three give evidence. What more do you require? What reply will you make? Why should eating meat make you unclean, if using such monstrosities in discussion does not? And, above all, the rays of the sun, which you surely think more of than all animal or vegetable food, have no smell or taste, and are remarkable among other substances only by their eminently bright

color; which is a loud call to you, and an obligation, despite yourselves, to place nothing higher than a bright color among the evidences of an admixture of good.

42. Thus you are forced into this difficulty, that you must acknowledge the part of God as dwelling more in blood, and in the filthy but bright-colored animal refuse which is thrown out in the streets, than in the pale leaves of the olive. If you reply, as you actually do, that olive leaves when burnt give out a flame, which proves the presence of light, while flesh when burnt does not, what will you say of oil, which lights nearly all the lamps in Italy? What of cow dung (which surely is more unclean than the flesh), which peasants use when dry as fuel, so that the fire is always at hand, and the liberation of the smoke is always going on? And if brightness and luster prove a greater presence of the divine part, why do you yourselves not purify it, why not appropriate it, why not liberate it? For it is found chiefly in flowers, not to speak of blood and countless things almost the same as blood in flesh or coming from it, and yet you cannot feed on flowers. And even if you were to eat flesh, you would certainly not take with your gruel the scales of fish, or some worms and flies, though these all shine with a light of their own in the dark.

43. What then remains, but that you should cease saying that you have in your eyes, nose, and palate sufficient means of testing the presence of the divine part in material objects? And, without these means, how can you tell not only that there is a greater part of God in plants than in flesh, but that there is any part in plants at all? Are you led to think this by their beauty—not the beauty of agreeable color, but that of agreement of parts? An excellent reason, in my opinion. For you will never

be so bold as to compare twisted pieces of wood with the bodies of animals, which are formed of members answering to one another. But if you choose the testimony of the senses, as those must do who cannot see with their mind the full force of existence, how do you prove that the substance of good escapes from bodies in course of time, and by some kind of attrition, but because God has gone out of it, according to your view, and has left one place for another? The whole is absurd. But, as far as I can judge, there are no marks or appearances to give rise to this opinion. For many things plucked from trees, or pulled out of the ground, are the better of some interval of time before we use them for food, as leeks and endive, lettuce, grapes, apples, figs, and some pears; and there are many other things which get a better color when they are not used immediately after being plucked, besides being more wholesome for the body, and having a finer flavor to the palate. But these things should not possess all these excellent and agreeable qualities, if, as you say, they become more destitute of good the longer they are kept after separation from their mother earth. Animal food itself is better and more fit for use the day after the animal is killed; but this should not be, if, as you hold, it possessed more good immediately after the slaughter than next day, when more of the divine substance had escaped.

44. Who does not know that wine becomes purer and better by age? Nor is it, as you think, more tempting to the destruction of the senses, but more useful for invigorating the body, —only let there be moderation, which ought to control everything. The senses are sooner destroyed by new wine. When the must has been only a short time in the vat, and has begun to ferment, it makes

those who look down into it fall headlong, affecting their brain, so that without assistance they would perish. And about health, everyone knows that bodies are swollen up and injuriously distended by new wine? Has it these bad properties because there is more good in it? Are they not found in wine when old because a good deal of the divine substance has gone? An absurd thing to say, especially for you, who prove the divine presence by the pleasing effect produced on your eyes, nose, and palate! And what a contradiction it is to make wine the poison of the princes of darkness, and yet to eat grapes! Has it more of the poison when in the cup than when in the cluster? Or if the evil remains unmixed after the good is gone, and that by the process of time, how is it that the same grapes, when hung up for awhile, become milder, sweeter, and more wholesome? or how does the wine itself, as already mentioned, become purer and brighter when the light has gone, and more wholesome by the loss of the beneficial substance?

45. What are we to say of wood and leaves, which in course of time become dry, but cannot be the worse on that account in your estimation? For while they lose that which produces smoke, they retain that from which a bright flame arises; and, to judge by the clearness, which you think so much of, there is more good in the dry than in the green. Hence you must either deny that there is more of God in the pure light than in the smoky one, which will upset all your evidences; or you must allow it to be possible that, when plants are plucked up, or branches plucked off, and kept for a time, more of the nature of evil may escape from them than of the nature of good. And, on the strength of this, we shall hold that more evil may go off from plucked fruits; and so more

good may remain in animal food. So much on the subject of time.

46. As for motion, and tossing, and rubbing, if these give the divine nature the opportunity of escaping from these substances, many things of the same kind are against you, which are improved by motion. In some grains the juice resembles wine, and is excellent when moved about. Indeed, as must not be overlooked, this kind of drink produces intoxication rapidly; and yet you never called the juice of grain the poison of the princes of darkness. There is a preparation of water, thickened with a little meal, which is the better of being shaken, and, strange to say, is lighter in color when the light is gone. The pastry cook stirs honey for a long time to give it this light color, and to make its sweetness milder and less unwholesome: you must explain how this can come from the loss of good. Again, if you prefer to test the presence of God by the agreeable effects on the hearing, and not sight, or smell, or taste, harps get their strings and pipes their bones from animals; and these become musical by being dried, and rubbed, and twisted. So the pleasures of music, which you hold to have come from the divine kingdom, are obtained from the refuse of dead animals, and that, too, when they are dried by time, and lessened by rubbing, and stretched by twisting. Such rough treatment, according to you, drives the divine substance from living objects; even cooking them, you say, does this. Why then are boiled thistles not unwholesome? Is it because God, or part of God, leaves them when they are cooked?

47. Why mention all the particulars, when it is difficult to enumerate them? Nor is it necessary; for everyone knows how many things are sweeter and more

wholesome when cooked. This ought not to be, if, as you suppose, things lose the good by being thus moved about. I do not suppose that you will find any proof from your bodily senses that flesh is unclean, and defiles the souls of those who eat it, because fruits, when plucked and shaken about in various ways, become flesh; especially as you hold that vinegar, in its age and fermentation, is cleaner than wine, and the mead you drink is nothing else than cooked wine, which ought to be more impure than wine, if material things lose the divine members by being moved about and cooked. But if not, you have no reason to think that fruits, when plucked, kept, handled, cooked, and digested, are forsaken by the good, and therefore supply most unclean matter for the formation of bodies.

48. But if it is not from their color and appearance, and smell and taste, that you think the good to be in these things, what else can you bring forward? Do you prove it from the strength and vigor which those things seem to lose when they are separated from the earth and put to use? If this is your reason (though its erroneousness is seen at once, from the fact that the strength of some things is increased after their separation from the earth, as in the case already mentioned of wine, which becomes stronger from age), —if the strength, then, is your reason, it would follow that the part of God is to be found in no food more abundantly than in flesh. For athletes, who especially require vigor and energy, are not in the habit of feeding on cabbage and fruit without animal food.

49. Is your reason for thinking the bodies of trees better than our bodies, that flesh is nourished by trees and not trees by flesh. You forget the obvious fact that plants, when manured with dung, become richer and more fertile

and crops heavier, though you think it your gravest charge against flesh that it is the abode of dung. This then gives nourishment to things you consider clean, though it is, according to you, the most unclean part of what you consider unclean. But if you dislike flesh because it springs from sexual intercourse, you should be pleased with the flesh of worms, which are bred in such numbers, and of such a size, in fruits, in wood, and in the earth itself, without any sexual intercourse. But there is some insincerity in this. For if you were displeased with flesh because it is formed from the cohabitation of father and mother, you would not say that those princes of darkness were born from the fruits of their own trees; for no doubt you think worse of these princes than of flesh, which you refuse to eat.

50. Your idea that all the souls of animals come from the food of their parents, from which confinement you pretend to liberate the divine substance which is held bound in your viands, is quite inconsistent with your abstinence from flesh, and makes it a pressing duty for you to eat animal food. For if souls are bound in the body by those who eat animal food, why do you not secure their liberation by being beforehand in eating the food? You reply, it is not from the animal food that the good part comes which those people bring into bondage, but from the vegetables which they take with their meat. What will you say then of the souls of lions, who feed only on flesh? They drink, is the reply, and so the soul is drawn in from the water and confined in flesh. But what of birds without number? What of eagles, which eat only flesh, and need no drink? Here you are at a loss, and can find no answer. For if the soul comes from food, and there are animals which neither drink anything nor have

any food but flesh, and yet bring forth young, there must be some soul in flesh; and you are bound to try your plan of purifying it by eating the flesh. Or will you say that a pig has a soul of light, because it eats vegetables, and drinks water; and that the eagle, because it eats only flesh, has a soul of darkness, though it is so fond of the sun?

51. What a confusion of ideas! What amazing fatuity! All this you would have escaped, if you had rejected idle fictions, and had followed what truth sanctions in abstinence from food, which would have taught you that sumptuous eating is to be avoided, not to escape pollution, as there is nothing of the kind, but to subdue the sensual appetite. For should anyone, from inattention to the nature of things, and the properties of the soul and body, allow that the soul is polluted by animal food, you will admit that it is much much more defiled by sensuality. Is it reasonable, then, or rather, is it not most unreasonable, to expel from the number of the elect a man who, perhaps for his health's sake, takes some animal food without sensual appetite; while, if a man eagerly devours peppered truffles, you can only reprove him for excess, but cannot condemn him as abusing your symbol? So one who has been induced, not by sensuality, but for health, to eat part of a fowl, cannot remain among your elect; though one may remain who has yielded voluntarily to an excessive appetite for comfits and cakes without animal matter. You retain the man plunged in the defilements of sensuality, and dismiss the man polluted, as you think, by the mere food; though you allow that the defilement of sensuality is far greater than that of meat. You keep hold of one who gloats with delight over highly-seasoned vegetables, unable to keep possession of himself; while you shut out one who, to satisfy hunger,

takes whatever comes, if suitable for nourishment, ready either to use the food, or to let it go. Admirable customs! Excellent morals! Notable temperance!

52. Again, the notion that it is unlawful for anyone but the elect to touch as food what is brought to your meals for what you call purification, leads to shameful and sometimes to criminal practices. For sometimes so much is brought that it cannot easily be eaten up by a few; and as it is considered sacrilege to give what is left to others, or, at least, to throw it away, you are obliged to eat to excess, from the desire to purify, as you call it, all that is given. Then, when you are full almost to bursting, you cruelly use force in making the boys of your sect eat the rest. So, it was charged against someone at Rome that he killed some poor children, by compelling them to eat for this superstitious reason. This I should not believe, did I not know how sinful you consider it to give this food to those who are not elect, or, at any rate, to throw it away. So the only way is to eat it; and this leads every day to gluttony, and may sometimes lead to murder.

53. For the same reason you forbid giving bread to beggars. By way of showing compassion, or rather of avoiding reproach, you advise to give money. The cruelty of this is equaled by its stupidity. For suppose a place where food cannot be purchased: the beggar will die of starvation, while you, in your wisdom and benevolence, have more mercy on a cucumber than on a human being! This is in truth (for how could it be better designated) pretended compassion, and real cruelty. Then observe the stupidity. What if the beggar buys bread for himself with the money you give him? Will the divine part, as you call it, not suffer the same in him when he buys the food as it would have suffered if he had taken it as a gift from you?

So, this sinful beggar plunges in corruption part of God eager to escape, and is aided in this crime by your money! But you in your great sagacity think it enough that you do not give to one about to commit murder a man to kill, though you knowingly give him money to procure somebody to be killed. Can any madness go beyond this? The result is, that either the man dies if he cannot get food for his money, or the food itself dies if he gets it. The one is true murder; the other what you call murder: though in both cases you incur the guilt of real murder. Again, there is the greatest folly and absurdity in allowing your followers to eat animal food, while you forbid them to kill animals. If this food does not defile, take it yourselves. If it defiles, what can be more unreasonable than to think it more sinful to separate the soul of a pig from its body than to defile the soul of a man with the pig's flesh.

Chapter 17. —Description of the Symbol of the Hands Among the Manichæans.

54. We must now notice and discuss the symbol of the hands. And, in the first place, your abstaining from the slaughter of animals and from injuring plants is shown by Christ to be mere superstition; for, because there is no community of rights between us and brutes and trees, He both sent the devils into a herd of swine, and withered by His curse a tree in which He had found no fruit. The swine assuredly had not sinned, nor had the tree. We are not so insane as to think that a tree is fruitful or barren by its own choice. Nor is it any reply to say that our Lord wished in these actions to teach some other truths; for everyone knows that. But assuredly the Son of God

would not commit murder to illustrate truth, if you call the destruction of a tree or of an animal murder. The signs which Christ wrought in the case of men, with whom we certainly have a community of rights, were in healing, not in killing them. And it would have been the same in the case of beasts and trees, if we had that community with them which you imagine.

55. I think it right to refer here to the authority of Scripture, because we cannot here enter on a profound discussion about the soul of animals, or the kind of life in trees. But as you preserve the right to call the Scriptures corrupted, in case you should find them too strongly opposed to you,—although you have never affirmed the passages about the tree and the herd of swine to be spurious,—still, lest someday you should wish to say this of them too, when you find how much they are against you, I will adhere to my plan, and will ask you, who are so liberal in your promises of evidence and truth, to tell me first what harm is done to a tree, I say not by plucking a leaf or an apple,—for which, however, one of you would be condemned at once as having abused the symbol, if he did it intentionally, and not accidentally,— but if you tear it up by the root. For the soul in trees, which, according to you, is a rational soul, is, in your theory, freed from bondage when the tree is cut down, —a bondage, too, where it suffered great misery and got no profit. For it is well known that you, in the words of your founder, threaten as a great, though not the greatest punishment, the change from a man to a tree; and it is not probable that the soul in a tree can grow in wisdom as it does in a man. There is the best reason for not killing a man, in case you should kill one whose wisdom or virtue might be of use to many, or one who might have attained

to wisdom, whether by the advice of another without himself, or by divine illumination in his own mind. And the more wisdom the soul has when it leaves the body, the more profitable is its departure, as we know both from well-grounded reasoning and from wide-spread belief. Thus, to cut down a tree is to set free the soul from a body in which it makes no progress in wisdom. You—the holy men, I mean—ought to be mainly occupied in cutting down trees, and in leading the souls thus emancipated to better things by prayers and psalms. Or can this be done only with the souls which you take into your belly, instead of aiding them by your understanding?

56. And you cannot escape the admission that the souls in trees make no progress in wisdom while they are there, when you are asked why no apostle was sent to teach trees as well as men, or why the apostle sent to men did not preach the truth to trees also. Your reply must be, that the souls while in such bodies cannot understand the divine precepts. But this reply lands you in great difficulties; for you declare that these souls can hear your voices and understand what you say, and see bodies and their motions, and even discern thoughts. If this is true, why could they learn nothing from the apostle of light? Why could they not learn even much better than we, since they can see into the mind? Your master, who, as you say, has difficulty in teaching you by speech, might have taught these souls by thought; for they could see his ideas in his mind before he expressed them. But if this is untrue, consider into what errors you have fallen.

57. As for your not plucking fruits or pulling up vegetables yourselves, while you get your followers to pluck and pull and bring them to you, that you may confer benefits not only on those who bring the food but on the

food which is brought, what thoughtful person can bear to hear this? For, first, it matters not whether you commit a crime yourself, or wish another to commit it for you. You deny that you wish this! How then can relief be given to the divine part contained in lettuce and leeks, unless someone pull them and bring them to the saints to be purified. And again, if you were passing through a field where the right of friendship permitted you to pluck anything you wished, what would you do if you saw a crow on the point of eating a fig? Does not, according to your ideas, the fig itself seem to address you and to beg of you piteously to pluck it yourself and give it burial in a holy belly, where it may be purified and restored, rather than that the crow should swallow it and make it part of his cursed body, and then hand it over to bondage and torture in other forms? If this is true, how cruel you are! If not, how silly! What can be more contrary to your opinions than to break the symbol? What can be unkinder to the member of God than to keep it?

58. This supposes the truth of your false and vain ideas. But you can be shown guilty of plain and positive cruelty flowing from the same error. For were any one lying on the road, his body wasted with disease, weary with journeying, and half-dead from his sufferings, and able only to utter some broken words, and if eating a pear would do him good as an astringent, and were he to beg you to help him as you passed by, and were he to implore you to bring the fruit from a neighboring tree, with no divine or human prohibition to prevent your doing so, while the man is sure to die for the want of it, you, a Christian man and a saint, will rather pass on and abandon a man thus suffering and entreating, lest the tree should lament the loss of its fruit, and you should be doomed to

Morals of the Manichaeans

the punishment threatened by Manichæus for breaking the symbol. Strange customs, and strange harmlessness!

59. Now, about killing animals, and the reasons for your opinion, much that has been said will apply also to this. For what harm will be done to the soul of a wolf by killing the wolf, since the wolf, as long as it lives, will be a wolf, and will not listen to any preacher, or give up, in the least, shedding the blood of sheep; and, by killing it, the rational soul, as you think, will be set free from its confinement in the body? But you make this slaughter unlawful even for your followers; for you think it worse than that of trees. And in this there is not much fault to be found with your senses, —that is, your bodily senses. For we see and hear by their cries that animals die with pain, although man disregards this in a beast, with which, as not having a rational soul, we have no community of rights. But as to your senses in the observation of trees, you must be entirely blind. For not to mention that there are no movements in the wood expressive of pain, what is clearer than that a tree is never better than when it is green and flourishing, gay with flowers, and rich in fruit? And this comes generally and chiefly from pruning. But if it felt the iron, as you suppose, it ought to die of wounds so many, so severe, instead of sprouting at the places, and reviving with such manifest delight.

60. But why do you think it a greater crime to destroy animals than plants, although you hold that plants have a purer soul than animals? There is a compensation, we are told, when part of what is taken from the fields is given to the elect and the saints to be purified. This has already been refuted; and it has, I think, been proved sufficiently that there is no reason for saying that more of the good part is found in vegetables than in flesh. But

should anyone support himself by selling butcher-meat, and spend the whole profit of his business in purchasing food for your elect, and bring larger supplies for those saints than any peasant or farmer, will he not plead this compensation as a warrant for his killing animals? But there is, we are told, some other mysterious reason; for a cunning man can always find some resource in the secrets of nature when addressing unlearned people. The story, then, is that the heavenly princes who were taken from the race of darkness and bound, and have a place assigned them in this region by the Creator of the world, have animals on the earth specially belonging to them, each having those coming from his own stock and class; and they hold the slaughterers of those animals guilty, and do not allow them to leave the earth, but harass them as much as they can with pains and torments. What simple man will not be frightened by this, and, seeing nothing in the darkness shrouding these things, will not think that the fact is as described? But I will hold to my purpose, with God's help, to rebut mysterious falsehood by the plainest truth.

61. Tell me, then, if animals on land and in water come in regular succession by ordinary generation from this race of princes, since the origin of animal life is traced to the abortive births in that race; —tell me, I say, whether bees and frogs, and many other creatures not sprung from sexual intercourse, may be killed with impunity. We are told they cannot. So, it is not because their relation to certain princes that you forbid your followers to kill animals. Or if you make a general relationship to all bodies, the princes would be equally concerned about trees, which you do not require your followers to spare. You are brought back to the weak

reply, that the injuries done in the case of plants are atoned for by the fruits which your followers bring to your church. For this implies that those who slaughter animals, and sell their flesh in the market, if they are your followers, and if they bring to you vegetables bought with their gains, may think nothing of the daily slaughter, and are cleared of any sin that may be in it by your repasts.

62. But if you say that, in order to expiate the slaughter, the thing must be given as food, as in the case of fruits and vegetables, —which cannot be done, because the elect do not eat flesh, and so your followers must not slaughter animals, —what reply will you give in the case of thorns and weeds, which farmers destroy in clearing their fields, while they cannot bring any food to you from them? How can there be pardon for such destruction, which gives no nourishment to the saints? Perhaps you also put away any sin committed, for the benefit of the fruits and vegetables, by eating some of these. What then if the fields are plundered by locusts, mice, or rats, as we see often happen? Can your rustic follower kill these with impunity, because he sins for the good of his crops? Here you are at a loss; for you either allow your followers to kill animals, which your founder prohibited, or you forbid them to be cultivators, which he made lawful. Indeed, you sometimes go so far as to say that a usurer is more harmless than a cultivator, —you feel so much more for melons than for men. Rather than hurt the melons, you would have a man ruined as a debtor. Is this desirable and praiseworthy justice, or not rather atrocious and damnable error? Is this commendable compassion, or not rather detestable barbarity?

63. What, again, of your not abstaining yourselves from the slaughter of lice, bugs, and fleas?

You think it a sufficient excuse for this to say that these are the dirt of our bodies. But this is clearly untrue of fleas and bugs; for everyone knows that these animals do not come from our bodies. Besides, if you abhor sexual intercourse as much as you pretend to do, you should think those animals all the cleaner which come from our bodies without any other generation; for although they produce offspring of their own, they are not produced in ordinary generation from us. Again, if we must consider as most filthy the production of living bodies, still worse must be the production of dead bodies. There must be less harm, therefore, in killing a rat, a snake, or a scorpion, which you constantly say come from our dead bodies. But to pass over what is less plain and certain, it is a common opinion regarding bees that they come from the carcasses of oxen; so there is no harm in killing them. Or if this too is doubted, everyone allows that beetles, at least, are bred in the ball of mud which they make and bury. You ought therefore to consider these animals, and others that it would be tedious to specify, more unclean than your lice; and yet you think it sinful to kill them, though it would be foolish not to kill the lice. Perhaps you hold the lice cheap because they are small. But if an animal is to be valued by its size, you must prefer a camel to a man.

64. Here we may use the gradation which often perplexed us when we were your followers. For if a flea may be killed because its small size, so may the fly which is bred in beans. And if this, so also may one of a little larger size, for its size at birth is even less. Then again, a bee may be killed, for its young is no larger than a fly. So on to the young of a locust, and to a locust; and then to the young of a mouse, and to a mouse. And, to cut short,

it is clear we may come at last to an elephant; so that one who thinks it no sin to kill a flea, because of its small size, must allow that it would be no sin in him to kill this huge creature. But I think enough has been said of these absurdities.

Chapter 18. —Of the Symbol of the Breast, and of the Shameful Mysteries of the Manichæans.

65. Lastly, there is the symbol of the breast, in which your very questionable chastity consists. For though you do not forbid sexual intercourse, you, as the apostle long ago said, forbid marriage in the proper sense, although this is the only good excuse for such intercourse. No doubt you will exclaim against this, and will make it a reproach against us that you highly esteem and approve perfect chastity, but do not forbid marriage, because your followers—that is, those in the second grade among you—can have wives. After you have said this with great noise and heat, I will quietly ask, Is it not you who hold that begetting children, by which souls are confined in flesh, is a greater sin than cohabitation? Is it not you who used to counsel us to observe as much as possible the time when a woman, after her purification, is most likely to conceive, and to abstain from cohabitation at that time, lest the soul should be entangled in flesh? This proves that you approve of having a wife, not for the procreation of children, but for the gratification of passion. In marriage, as the marriage law declares, the man and woman come together for the procreation of children. Therefore, whoever makes the procreation of children a greater sin than copulation, forbids marriage, and makes the woman not a wife, but a mistress, who for

some gifts presented to her is joined to the man to gratify his passion. Where there is a wife there must be marriage. But there is no marriage where motherhood is not in view; therefore neither is there a wife. In this way you forbid marriage. Nor can you defend yourselves successfully from this charge, long ago brought against you prophetically by the Holy Spirit.

66. Moreover, when you are so eager in your desire to prevent the soul from being confined in flesh by conjugal intercourse, and so eager in asserting that the soul is set free from seed by the food of the saints, do you not sanction, unhappy beings, the suspicion entertained about you? For why should it be true regarding corn and beans and lentils and other seeds, that when you eat them you wish to set free the soul, and not true of the seeds of animals? For what you say of the flesh of a dead animal, that it is unclean because there is no soul in it, cannot be said of the seed of the animal; for you hold that it keeps confined the soul which will appear in the offspring, and you avow that the soul of Manichæus himself is thus confined. And as your followers cannot bring these seeds to you for purification, who will not suspect that you make this purification secretly among yourselves, and hide it from your followers, in case they should leave you? If you do not these things, as it is to be hoped you do not, still you see how open to suspicion your superstition is, and how impossible it is to blame men for thinking what your own profession suggests, when you maintain that you set free souls from bodies and from senses by eating and drinking. I wish to say no more about this: you see yourselves what room there is here for denunciation. But as the matter is one rather to repress than to invite remark, and also as throughout my

discourse my purpose appears of exaggerating nothing, and of keeping to bare facts and arguments, we shall pass on to other matters.

Chapter 19. —Crimes of the Manichæans.

67. We see then, now, the nature of your three symbols. These are your customs. This is the end of your notable precepts, in which there is nothing sure, nothing steadfast, nothing consistent, nothing irreproachable, but all doubtful, or rather undoubtedly and entirely false, all contradictory, abominable, absurd. In a word, evil practices are detected in your customs so many and so serious, that one wishing to denounce them all, if he were at all able to enlarge, would require at least a separate treatise for each. Were you to observe these, and to act up to your profession, no childishness, or folly, or absurdity would go beyond yours; and when you praise and teach these things without doing them, you display craft and deceit and malevolence equal to anything that can be described or imagined.

68. During nine full years that I attended you with great earnestness and assiduity, I could not hear of one of your elect who was not found transgressing these precepts, or at least was not suspected of doing so. Many were caught at wine and animal food, many at the baths; but this we only heard by report. Some were proved to have seduced other men's wives, so that in this case I could not doubt the truth of the charge. But suppose this, too, a report rather than a fact. I myself saw, and not I only, but others who have either escaped from that superstition, or will, I hope, yet escape, —we saw, I say, in a square in Carthage, on a road much frequented, not

one, but more than three of the elect walking behind us, and accosting some women with such indecent sounds and gestures as to outdo the boldness and insolence of all ordinary rascals. And it was clear that this was quite habitual, and that they behaved in this way to one another, for no one was deterred by the presence of a companion, showing that most of them, if not all, were affected with this evil tendency. For they did not all come from one house, but lived in quite different places, and quite accidentally left together the place where they had met. It was a great shock to us, and we lodged a complaint about it. But who thought of inflicting punishment, —I say not by separation from the church, but even by severe rebuke in proportion to the heinousness of the offence?

69. All the excuse given for the impunity of those men was that, at that time, when their meetings were forbidden by law, it was feared that the persons suffering punishment might retaliate by giving information. What then of their assertion that they will always have persecution in this world, for which they suppose that they will be thought the more of? for this is the application they make of the words about the world hating them. And they will have it that truth must be sought for among them, because, in the promise of the Holy Spirit, the Paraclete, it is said that the world cannot receive Him. This is not the place to discuss this question. But clearly, if you are always to be persecuted, even to the end of the world, there will be no end to this laxity, and to the unchecked spread of all this immorality, from your fear of giving offence to men of this character.

70. This answer was also given to us, when we reported to the very highest authorities that a woman had complained to us that in a meeting, where she was along

with other women, not doubting of the sanctity of these people, some of the elect came in, and when one of them had put out the lamp, one, whom she could not distinguish, tried to embrace her, and would have forced her into sin, had she not escaped by crying out. How common must we conclude the practice to have been which led to the misdeed on this occasion! And this was done on the night when you keep the feast of vigils. Forsooth, besides the fear of information being given, no one could bring the offender before the bishop, as he had so well guarded against being recognized. As if all who entered along with him were not implicated in the crime; for in their indecent merriment they all wished the lamp to be put out.

71. Then what wide doors were opened for suspicions, when we saw them full of envy, full of covetousness, full of greed for costly foods, constantly at strife, easily excited about trifles! We concluded that they were not competent to abstain from the things they professed to abstain from, if they found an opportunity in secret or in the dark. There were two of sufficiently good character, of active minds, and leaders in their debates, with whom we had a more particular and intimate acquaintance than with the rest. One of them was much associated with us, because he was also engaged in liberal studies; he is said to be now an elder there. These two were very jealous of one another, and one accused the other—not openly, but in conversation, as he had opportunity, and in whispers—of having made a criminal assault on the wife of one of the followers. He again, in clearing himself to us, brought the same charge against another of the elect, who lived with this follower as his most trusted friend. He had, going in suddenly, caught

this man with the woman, and his enemy and rival had advised the woman and her paramour to raise this false report about him, that he might not be believed if he gave any information. We were much distressed, and took it greatly to heart, that although there was a doubt about the assault on the woman, the jealous feeling in those two men, than whom we found none better in the place, showed itself so keenly, and inevitably raised a suspicion of other things.

72. Another thing was, that we very often saw in theatres men belonging to the elect, men of years and, it was supposed, of character, along with a hoary-headed elder. We pass over the youths, whom we used to come upon quarrelling about the people connected with the stage and the races; from which we may safely conclude how they would be able to refrain in secret, when they could not subdue the passion by which they were exposed in the eyes of their followers, bringing on them disgrace and flight. In the case of the saint, whose discussions we attended in the street of the fig-sellers, would his atrocious crime have been discovered if he had been able to make the dedicated virgin his wife without making her pregnant? The swelling womb betrayed the secret and unthought-of iniquity. When her brother, a young man, heard of it from his mother, he felt keenly the injury, but refrained, from regard to religion, from a public accusation. He succeeded in getting the man expelled from that church, for such conduct cannot always be tolerated; and that the crime might not be wholly unpunished, he arranged with some of his friends to have the man well beaten and kicked. When he was thus assailed, he cried out that they should spare him, from regard to the authority of the opinion of Manichæus, that

Adam the first hero had sinned, and was a greater saint after his sin.

73. This, in fact, is your notion about Adam and Eve. It is a long story; but I will touch only on what concerns the present matter. You say that Adam was produced from his parents, the abortive princes of darkness; that he had in his soul the most part of light, and very little of the opposite race. So while he lived a holy life, because the prevalence of good, still the opposite part in him was stirred up, so that he was led away into conjugal intercourse. Thus he fell and sinned, but afterwards lived in greater holiness. Now, my complaint is not so much about this wicked man, who, under the garb of an elect and holy man, brought such shame and reproach on a family of strangers by his shocking immorality. I do not charge you with this. Let it be attributed to the abandoned character of the man, and not to your habits. I blame the man for the atrocity, and not you. Still there is this in you all that cannot, as far as I can see, be admitted or tolerated, that while you hold the soul to be part of God, you still maintain that the mixture of a little evil prevailed over the superior force and quantity of good. Who that believes this, when incited by passion, will not find here an excuse, instead of checking and controlling his passion?

Chapter 20. —Disgraceful Conduct Discovered at Rome.

74. What more shall I say of your customs? I have mentioned what I found myself when I was in the city when the things were done. To go through all that happened at Rome in my absence would take a long time.

I will, however, give a short account of it; for the matter became so notorious, that even the absent could not remain in ignorance of it. And when I was afterwards in Rome, I ascertained the truth of all I had heard, although the story was told me by an eye-witness whom I knew so well and esteemed so highly, that I could not feel any doubt about it. One of your followers, then, quite equal to the elect in their far-famed abstinence, for he was both liberally educated, and was in the habit of defending your sect with great zeal, took it very ill that he had cast in his teeth the vile conduct of the elect, who lived in all kinds of places, and went hither and thither for lodging of the worst description. He therefore desired, if possible, to assemble all who were willing to live according to the precepts into his own house, and to maintain them at his own expense; for he was above the average in carelessness as to spending money, besides being above the average in the amount he had to spend. He complained that his efforts were hindered by the remissness of the bishops, whose assistance he required for success. At last one of your bishops was found, —a man, as I know, very rude and unpolished, but somehow, from his very moroseness, the more inclined to strict observance of morality. The follower eagerly lays hold of this man as the person he had long wished for and found at last, and relates his whole plan. He approves and assents, and agrees to be the first to take up his abode in the house. When this was done, all the elect who could be at Rome were assembled there. The rule of life in the epistle of Manichæus was laid before them. Many thought it intolerable, and left; not a few felt ashamed, and stayed. They began to live as they had agreed, and as this high authority enjoined. The follower all the time was zealously enforcing everything on everybody, though never, in any case, what he did not undertake himself. Meanwhile quarrels constantly arose among the elect. They charged one another with crimes, all which he lamented to hear, and managed to make them unintentionally expose one another in their altercations. The revelations were vile beyond description. Thus, appeared the true character of those who were unlike the rest in being willing to bend to the yoke of the precepts. What then is to be suspected, or rather, concluded, of the others? To come to a close, they gathered together on one occasion and complained that they could not keep the regulations. Then came rebellion. The follower stated his case most concisely, that either all must be kept, or the man who had given such a sanction to such precepts, which no one could fulfill, must be thought a great fool. But, as was inevitable, the wild clamor of the mob prevailed over the opinion of one man. The bishop himself gave way at last, and took to flight with great disgrace; and he was said to have got in provisions by stealth, contrary to rule, which were often discovered. He had a supply of money from his private purse, which he carefully kept concealed.

75. If you say these things are false, you contradict what is too clear and public. But you may say so if you like. For, as the things are certain, and easily known by those who wish to know them, those who deny that they are true show what their habit of telling the truth is. But you have other replies with which I do not find fault. For you either say that some do keep your precepts, and that they should not be mixed up with the guilty in condemning the others; or that the whole inquiry into the character of the members of your sect is wrong, for the

question is of the character of the profession. Should I grant both of these (although you can neither point out those faithful observers of the precepts, nor clear your heresy of all those frivolities and iniquities), still I must insist on knowing why you heap reproaches on Christians of the Catholic name on seeing the immoral life of some, while you either have the effrontery to repel inquiry about your members, or the still greater effrontery not to repel it, wishing it to be understood that in your scanty membership there are some unknown individuals who keep the precepts they profess, but that among the multitudes in the Catholic Church there are none.

www.ingramcontent.com/pod-product-compliance
Lightning Source LLC
Chambersburg PA
CBHW052117070526
44584CB00017B/2525